Radical
Immediate
Retirement

Radical Immediate Retirement

ESCAPE THE SOUL CRUSHING HORROR OF YOUR JOB **RIGHT NOW!**

DAVID DOWNIE

Radical Immediate Retirement: ESCAPE THE SOUL CRUSHING HORROR OF YOUR JOB RIGHT NOW!

See other books by the Author at his Amazon author page:
www.amazon.com/author/bestsellers

Published by Blue Peg Publishing

If you have purchased the ebook version of this book, then please consider buying the print version if your family enjoys the ebook.

Contents

ABOUT THE AUTHOR

David Downie is the founder of AustralianBeers.com and the Australian contributor to the international beer bible *1001 Beers You Must Drink Before You Die*. He was profiled in the book *Three Sheets to the Wind* by leading UK beer expert Pete Brown.

David is also the author of 2 books on contract law and 6 illustrated children's books, some of which have been translated into over 40 languages. He assisted the author of the *Macquarie Book of Slang* with several of its less salubrious definitions.

David has honors degrees in both science and law and is a former Partner at a major Australian law firm.

David has appeared on Sky News and has been quoted by publications including the Australian Financial Review, Business Review Weekly and the Sydney Morning Herald as an expert in law, children's books, beer and Australian culture. The BBC asked to interview him about a light version of VB, but he declined as he refused to drink it.

David Radically and Immediately Retired forever at age 38 and now spends his time as he chooses.

FAQ – DEFENSIVE WORKERS READ THIS

Is Radical Immediate Retirement (RIR) for you? If you have made the choice to seek out this book and read this far, then chances are it is. After all, what's the worst thing that can happen? That you take up your old slog? Big deal. The potential upside for your life is enormous.

Do I have to be rich?

Not at all. This mindset works regardless of how much you are worth (as money is only a small part of the equation, and optional at that). But you probably have more cash than you realize.

Do I have to be burnt out?

No! But to be honest you probably are, a bit, even if you think you aren't.

Will my working friends still love me if I am retired?

Of course they will. Chances are they will be more curious than critical. Whether or not you still love them once you enter the world of immediate retirement and have all the time in the world to watch their crazy antics is another question.

Do I need to join a bowls club and watch TV like grandpa?

Only if you want to. But if you continue to do this after you recover from work induced burnout then I suspect you won't have the gumption to immediately retire in the first place.

Do I have to live in my car and fish for food?

I don't know anyone who does. But if someone did for a couple of months with their tanned girlfriend off a beach in South America, would that be so bad?

How would that compare with your cubicle life?

A RADICAL
PERSPECTIVE

*These people may truly be said to be in the pure
state of nature, and may appear to some to be
the most wretched upon the earth; but in reality
they are far happier than ... we Europeans.*

Captain James Cook's observation on
aboriginal Australians, 1770

*First commentaries from Joseph Banks and
James Cook stressed that they were far more
happy than Europeans "because far removed
from the anxieties attendant on riches."*

Alister Davidson, The Invisible State:
The Formation of the Australian State, 1991

*I do not hesitate to declare that the natives of New South
Wales possess a considerable portion of that acumen,
or sharpness of intellect, which bespeaks genius. All
savages hate [white man's] toil, and place happiness
in [what the white man would consider] inaction...*

Walkin Tench, 1788

Think, for a moment, not about what makes you happy, but
what makes you unhappy - with your life; right now. Chances
are part of your sorrow stems from having to get up at 6.30

every morning before travelling to someone else's business where you spend all day interacting with people you dislike doing mind numbing or stressful work. Or perhaps a good part of burden flows from your mortgage or rent, which must be paid every single week of your existence lest you end up 'homeless.'

For some it is simply the pain of not having the freedom to do what they want, when they want, especially during their most vibrant and exhilarating years.

What, in turn, enters your mind when you think of the happiest moments of your life so far? The warmth of your mother's embrace as a child? Sitting in the afternoon sun, feet up, as you gaze out over the sea? Laughter with partner as you cuddle in the grass? Or perhaps getting really good at something you enjoy, and helping other people as a result of your skill.

How would you spend your last day on Earth?

Strangely enough, if you consider the life of the Australian aboriginal pre-white settlement, and indeed any culture at one with nature, few if any of those unhappy, relatively modern worries exist. They had no mortgage. No rent. No workplace of pain. But, as the white interlopers observed, they had all of the deepest pleasures you could imagine — company, comfort, warmth, laughter, personal satisfaction from being good at things....

If you live according to the dictates of nature,
you will never be poor; if according to the
notions of man, you will never be rich.

Seneca (4 B.C.-A.D 65)

*A man is rich in proportion to the number
of things he can afford to let alone.*

Henry Thoreau, 1854

Where did civilization go wrong? How is it the majority of us spend the best years of our lives in jobs we don't enjoy to pay for assets we don't really use? At what point exactly did we start thinking that happiness does not come from a lazy swim at the sea on a hot day, or a lover's embrace, but rather from spending most of our time working for shiny trinkets we wouldn't even know about if we hadn't seen them advertised?

Of course for most it is not practical or advisable to try and live as the ancients did. People today (including modern Australian aboriginals) lack the skill and access to the physical environment and social support that makes this lifestyle feasible. What's more, undeniably there are some modern pleasures that aren't merely money sucking trinkets – like medicine and access to ideas on the internet...

But it's food for thought isn't it? If we know that a life filled with freedom and simple pleasures brings so much more happiness than the life of the time-poor wage slave (or shipmate), then can't we, as intelligent people, use this to our advantage?

YOU ARE ALREADY A MILLIONAIRE

Greed is a reason why people work more than they have to. They want all the pleasures money can buy; to live like a millionaire. But what does it mean, to live like a millionaire – a rock star even?

Well, that depends on when you were born.

There is an old interview with John Lennon on YouTube, which shows him in the back of one of his luxury cars. The 1960s style voice over tells the audience that "Only a Beatle" could have a black and white TV in the back of his car.

That's right. Only a Beatle – a rock star – a millionaire.

So up until very recently (perhaps 10 years ago), not only could a Beatle not afford the technology that you probably have in your pocket, but nobody could. Not Bill Gates. Not Warren Buffet. Not NASA. Nobody.

If you have a smart phone, you have more and cooler 'stuff' than the richest guy in the world for almost all of human history.

Louis XV of France – a king no less – died of smallpox, despite his millions, a disease you won't be dying of any time soon because it has been wiped out by science.[1]

You won't die of an infection next time you scratch yourself, because you can pay a few dollars or less to save yourself using technology (antibiotics) that the richest person in the world prior to the 1940s couldn't have accessed.

Back in the 1970s it cost the same to fly to England as it did to buy a house. In the 1980s no normal person flew – only the rich. Nowadays it costs more to drive and flying is available to pretty well everyone.

Australia's longest serving Prime Minister fretted for days before his first international phone call in the 1960s – it was such a big deal, and only available to him and his ilk at that time (at a mind blowing cost).[2]

Anyway you look at it – no matter how much money you have - you are richest guy or gal in the *world* in terms of the cool things you can buy and the medicine you can access, by even the standards of *10 years ago*, let alone the 200,000 years that humans have been eyeing off each other's stuff.

And some people want to ruin their lives working to have more?

---

[1] Louis was one of five reigning monarchs who died of smallpox. It is estimated to have killed from 300-500 million people in the 20th century.
[2] Check out *Letters for my Daughter* by Robert Menzies if interested.

THE MINIMUM EFFECTIVE DOSE FOR THE GOOD LIFE?

That man is rich whose pleasures are the cheapest....
Money is not required to buy one necessity of the soul.

Henry Thoreau, 1854

He is a king who desires nothing.

Seneca (4 B.C.-A.D 65)

If running around working our asses off to buy stuff that makes us richer than the millionaires of the past is a greedy waste of time, then why *do* we work at all? What money do we need to live the good life then?

Good question.

The answer is we don't need very much at all.

One fellow – who, I might say, does sound a little radical even to me, decided that all he needed was one set of clothes and a backpack. That's it. He then just quit his job as a bank teller, and set out walking in 1977.

He walked around the highways and side roads of Australia. When he found a shoe (always an odd one) he put it in his backpack as a spare. He found change on the side of the road. He camped in beautiful bush settings. He met other wanderers on the road.

He kept walking for 36 years (apart from 3 months when he cared for his dying father). He's still walking.[3]

That sounds crazy but there's no doubt that he's happier (and healthier) than he would be had he stayed working as a bank teller, spending his money on stuff that clearly he doesn't need.

That was his form of immediate retirement.

Although this shows what is possible (and indeed, that there is no reason or excuse for suffering work misery for one more second) most of us will want more, and indeed can have it.

Housing

There is no more fatal blunderer than he who consumes the greater part of his life getting his living.

Henry Thoreau, 1854

We do need somewhere to live. Does it need to be a $500,000 house that takes the average person 25 years (the best 25 years no less) of their lives to pay off?

No way. That's insane.

---

[3] See http://www.abc.net.au/local/audio/2014/03/05/3957316.htm for an interview.

Happiness does not come from paying off a mansion for 25 years. Personally one of the happiest times in my life was spent living in a converted delivery van. All you need is a bed and a door. My girlfriend and I spent over 8 months driving from place to place.

We got to know each other better. We relaxed. We got fitter. We smiled more. It was wonderful, and, oh, about 1000 times better than working full time in a job to pay for some ego-sized house that you might not even live to see paid off.

Along the way we saw all sorts of alternative housing with all sorts of happy people living there. Much happier than the corporate zombies we were familiar with.

People lived in demountables by the sea, spending their days fishing and yarning over a beer and a BBQ. Some people lived for free in tents in beautiful places, even with little ones.

Others lived in cheap apartments. We spoke to travellers who had bought houses internationally for bargain prices. Just because you live in a bubble area with locals who don't know any better doesn't mean you have to. Beware of local wisdom - of living as your parents lived. The world has changed and blindly doing as everyone does is more a sign of you taking the wrong direction than the right one.

What old people say you cannot do, you
try and find that you can. Old deeds for
old people, and new deeds for new.

Henry Thoreau, 1854

Of course, you don't have to buy. Many rent. More houses than not globally can be rented for less than $80 per week. Rooms cost less. Sometimes you can find accommodation for free (by housesitting for example – it's easy to find somewhere using online sites). There are many, many options. The laziest, most inefficient option is to buy a mansion like all of your friends and become enslaved to your employer for decades as a result.

How boring.

Food

Even Epicurus, the teacher of pleasure, used to observe stated intervals, during which he satisfied his hunger in stingy fashion; he wished to see whether he thereby fell short of full and complete happiness, and, if so, by what amount be fell short, and whether this amount was worth purchasing at the price of great effort.

Seneca (4 B.C.-A.D 65)

Food is both a problem to be solved and also a potential source of enormous pleasure for someone seeking immediate retirement. Learn to cook. Plant a garden. The more skilled you are the less food will cost and the better it will be. This is a principle more broadly applicable to every problem in your life that needs to be solved: the more skilled you are the more efficiently you will be able to solve the problem and the better the outcome will be.

To only solve problems using money is lazy and inefficient. And the solution will often be inelegant and suboptimal. Take a meal for example. If you eat out, chances are you will get an expensive, crappy meal. Cooking a banquet for yourself and your partner can be done for under $10 (less in many parts of the world) and be a beautiful healthy experience. Plus you get the pleasure of initially learning the skill of cooking and then applying it to everyone's delight.

That is how you should treat your life: acquiring new skills that allow you to solve more problems and live more efficiently.

One recent example involved my brother hosting a feast for 40 people. How would you go about this? Get professional caterers in at $50 a head? (At a cost of $2,000) Or would you say, no I could cook, and buy 40 steaks (at 7 bucks a pop - $280) along with some salads and the rest?

What my brother did was to draw on his experience in travelling South America, where he saw cordero al asador being cooked – google it.[4] It's a striking, amazing sight of a whole lamb or sheep being cooked over a wood fire on, wait for it, a crucifix. They skin the beast, gut it, and stick the crucifix near the open flame where it is turned every now and then for, say, 8 hours. A special, home made garlic sauce is applied for moisture and flavor.

The result: an amazing, melt-in-your-mouth tender lamb dish, along with a spectacle the likes of which your guests have never seen and will remember forever.

Sounds impossible to do in the west? Well, if you are clueless, or I should more correctly say, skilless, it is. But my brother drew on his work related experience to weld up a

---

[4]   http://www.google.com.au/search?client=safari&rls=en&q=cordero+al+asad
or&ie=UTF-8&oe=UTF-8&gfe_rd=cr&ei=0ZDdU9GqFcqN8QfB3IG4AQ

crucifix, and bought a whole lamb from a farmer (at a cost of just over $100). He then used hardwood he had chopped himself on his property to get the fire, and the talking point of the party, going.

It was a smashing success.

Great, you say, but I can't weld. Plus how do you buy a beast if you don't have any cash? Wrong questions. You're a problem solver. You're smarter than you think – you just aren't used to using your brain to solve problems in your own life. Instead you save all of your brains for the *least* important part of your life – your work.

Use your brains to solve your own problems first, not other people's. Everyone has experience. Everyone has skills. Everyone has some sort of opportunity or advantage. What are they? Use them! Develop them!

In this instance, my brother could have raised the beast himself (although a live one only costs $30 - he could have invited a butcher to the party to do the dirty work). My brother's skills include chopping wood, which is expensive. He could have chopped his own wood and sold it to raise cash for the beast, or he could have chopped wood for the farmer himself.

His father-in-law had just shot and slaughtered a water buffalo the weekend prior. He could have worked something out with him – or better still, learned from him how to do it himself so he didn't need any help in the future.

He could have also.... what? If you're smart enough to have read this far, you're smart enough to offer him a few options.

And if you can offer him options, then you can offer yourself some. And implement them.

The point is to transform the experience from a Bill Gate's style expensive, point-and-click exercise in consumption and grandstanding, to a look-at-this-beast-I-procured-for-stuff-all-and-cooked-on-a-crucifix-I-welded-myself-for-the-best-damn-party-you've-ever-been-to.

Which is the more enjoyable? Could Bill Gates pay for the fun you would get doing this? Money is only one part of the equation – usually the most boring part. There is little pleasure to be had lying back in a chair, obese and listless, and yelling out instructions to your suppliers (who generally scorn you behind your back).

That's no way to live.

And the best part? If you don't exist like a bloated slob, pointing and paying, then you can reduce your cost of living to something extremely efficient, and then use your big brain to work out how to come up with the small amount of money that is needed, either through a return on capital, commercialization of fun activities, a low stress automated lifestyle business, and so on.

It's a million times better than a million dollars.

The Internet

Everyone is different, but if you're like me you want to have a good internet connection. This gives you access to ideas and information and often allows you live a location independent lifestyle by letting you run your affairs from anywhere. It is also the source of endless entertainment....

But I need cash to have the internet you cry! Must work 9-5 7 days a week in the horror for 40 years to pay for it!

Do you? Think of this again like another problem to solve (that's right, just like you solve problems for your boss). Imagine you are helping out a simple friend. How would you get internet access for him? Surely you can come up with some options. Now imagine your friend is as smart as you are – would that increase his choices?

While it depends on your circumstances a starting point is to look at free internet in libraries and cafes (and sometimes just as you walk along a row of apartments...). Many parts of the world also have very low cost providers if you search them out.

Treat it as a challenge, smart boy.

Health (Care)

> *Health is the greatest gift, contentment*
> *is the greatest wealth.*

> Buddha – circa 500 BC

> *What can be added to the happiness of a man who is*
> *in health, out of debt, and has a clear conscience?*

> Adam Smith (1723-1790)

It is said that two thirds of health problems are caused by stress, a poor diet and lack of exercise. In my experience each of these conditions is caused in a large part by a poor lifestyle – meaning working as a wage-slave all day!

The insanity is that people justify keeping this poor lifestyle because of their 'need' to pay for health insurance. If someone paid you to smoke and you kept doing it so you would get the best care when you got lung cancer – would you keep puffing away?

No, it's madness.

If you want a good health outcome, START by getting healthy – not paying for insurance against the problems you are bringing on yourself. If you are overweight, it's a freaking emergency. If you are stressed out, it's a freaking emergency. If you are eating processed sugary crap, then it's a freaking emergency.

It's like stopping smoking before worrying about lung cancer insurance. Just stop! Then worry about the insurance.

Once you've done that (quit the job making you sick), and spend, say, 6 months or a year (or more) getting healthy again, then you should worry about 'health care'. Your own care is far more important than any you can buy. Outsourcing a fix after it's too late is a symptom of a broader cultural trait of paying other people to solve your problems for you. Health is *your problem*, which must be solved first – by you. Once that is solved – using all means necessary - then you can think about how to pay for insurance.

Insurance isn't hard. People do it all over the world. Move to somewhere with 'free' health care and become a citizen.

Find a cheaper plan or care (looking globally). You're smart. Work it out like you work everything out.

Don't use insurance as an excuse to stay trapped in health-ruining horror for the best years of your life.

Youth

Youth is wasted on the young

Oscar Wild (1856-1950)

Everyone wants to be young again. The truth is, if you are young (or even just younger than the next fellow) you hold riches greater than the wealthiest older person.

Do you think that Bill Gates wouldn't give all of his fortune back to be 25 once more? Of course he would. Same with Steve Jobs, Bill Clinton and every single old retired rich guy you see as you travel the world once you have quit your job.

Every one of them would give every single penny to get back even 10 years of their lives.

The price of anything is the amount
of life you exchange for it.

Henry Thoreau, 1854

So really, once again you are rich beyond reckoning. You have something that is beyond money. It is quite literally priceless because it cannot be bought. There are many aspects of life like this. Often such treasures are ignored by the rich because of their focus on earning and consumption (how tired), and the fact that they are often old and unhealthy and don't want to let on that their wealth is nothing by comparison.

Indeed youth is a big reason to have a smile on your face as you enjoy your life without participating on the treadmill.

TAKING STOCK
AND MAKING THE
HARD DECISIONS

The mass of men lead lives of quiet desperation.

Henry Thoreau, 1854

It is difficult to free fools from the chains they revere.

Voltaire, 1694-1778

Before you RIR (Radically and Immediately Retire, remember?) you need to look honestly at where you stand from a financial, skill and health perspective. Of course retirement depends on all three of these – not just money (which is what your financial planner would have you believe).[5]

Financially you should consider the market value of everything you own (less your debts). That means *everything*, including your shitty (or glitzy) car AND your prized home (if you own one). It is worth looking at your home in particular, as that tends to be the most emotional of a person's assets as well as the biggest money sink.

Yes, I know all of your friends have a house. Yes, I know that 'losing the home' is the biggest financial fear of most. But if

---

[5] Is he retired?

you want to escape the nightmare, you've got to take a good hard look at yourself - as though you were advising yourself professionally. The problem – how to stop work immediately and only do the things that bring you satisfaction. The solution? Well, the solution might just involve your house.

What would you tell your friend who wanted to give up work if he had, say, a $500,000 mortgage and was paying it off with a $75,000 salary? It would be pretty darn obvious wouldn't it?

He would sell the house, kill the debt, take the cash and solve the housing problem another way wouldn't he?

Or perhaps he (or you!) could rent the house out? If you can rent the house out for say $25,000 a year, and have over $20,000 clear after expenses and taxes, then, guess what, if you can live on $20,000 a year then YOU ARE COMPLETELY RETIRED AND NEVER HAVE TO WORK AGAIN FOR MONEY.

That's outrageous, you think. You could never live on $20,000 a year.

Couldn't you? Almost every single person in the history of the world does. Most people alive at this very moment do. To them you would be a pension carrying millionaire.

Are you that greedy that you aren't happy living on an income that is greater than almost every person alive (when looking at things globally)?

Are you that *inefficient?*

Think for a moment. It's 400 bucks a week. *You wouldn't have to work on things you didn't want to work on.* You could live at a beach resort that allowed camping forever on that amount. You could share a room. You could live in an RV or a tent. You could live in many lower cost countries easily on that amount. Like a rich person.

If you applied the sort of brain power that you clearly had to be able to pay the house off to living on 400 bucks a week don't you think you could?

This is in effect what most of the early retirement crowd out there encourage you to do: save enough cash and invest it (typically in shares) so that the expected returns are enough for you to live off forever. What's attractive about the combination of simple (efficient) living and saving the vast bulk of your salary is that if you are disciplined enough you can reach financial independence in as little as 5 years.

One of the giant brains out there who has been hugely influential to many is a fellow by the name of Jacob Fisker of www.earlyretirementextreme.com. He was working as a theoretical physicist (really) when he tired of it all and saved enough to retire forever some time after 3% of his investments covered his living expenses of $7,000 per year. He was 33 years of age when he retired.

Among other things Jacob has used his math brain to assert that a 3% withdrawal rate from your investments is likely to be sustainable over a lifetime (meaning that you shouldn't run out of money and inflation is covered). In other words, if you can save 25 times of your annual living expenses then you will be ok ($175,000 in his case).

The paradox of this well meaning fellow is that no later than two years after he 'retired', and having published some wonderful articles and a dense textbook about the freedom of not working in a cubicle for a living, he promptly went back to full time work in the financial sector! He has remained there for some years now.

That doesn't detract from his writings though, and you should seek them out regardless of the approach you take. While his life is his to lead, it's comforting that he has retained his financial independence (which perhaps is a better word than retirement when you swap one full time cubicle career for another), in the sense his expenses are more than covered by his passive income. He can literally do what he wants, and if what he wants to do (for now) provides him with cash then good for him!

Comparison with traditional early retirement

In fact, that's the difference between the classic early retirement approach and Radical Immediate Retirement. Early retirees will typically tell you what everyone tells you – save money for retirement. They will also tell you to spend less. The more you save (and invest) and the less you spend the faster you will be able to live off your investments and retire to do as you will.

RIR, on the other hand, doesn't involve any further capital accumulation (saving money in the hellhole for years). It's about getting out right now.

It may well be that when you stop and consider what capital you have accumulated over your working life you are surprised with the outcome (the capital in your home for instance, when used as an investment rather than a money sink).

But regardless of what money you have, if any, if you have any spark in you whatsoever you are likely not to spend your life vegetating or playing golf. Instead you are going to do what takes your fancy. And if you are clever enough to have sought out this book, then chances are that deep down you are an interested and capable person who is going to use his or her new found freedom to do some extremely cool stuff.

Some of that activity is likely to be income producing. The less money you have invested, and the less efficient you are at living, the more desirable an income producing activity will be. But in the most part, it is likely that you will just follow your interests, and commercialization opportunities will present themselves. In effect you will be learning new skills, having fun, and doing things that you get a jolly out of doing. It might be spending one day a week looking after guide dog puppies. It might be writing an ebook about pelicans you have rescued, or your year volunteering for board in the French countryside.

It could even be working in the finance sector – if you have an enormous and peculiar brain and enjoy that sort of thing. Or better still, starting an online business that gives you pleasure (in a boss and systems kind of way) – designing the whole thing from the ground up as being something that doesn't demand much of your time.[6]

Either way, you have escaped the nightmare grind, freed yourself by living as efficiently as you have to given your skills

---

[6]   This is the model of the Four Hour Work Week by Tim Ferris.

and resources, and spending your time free to do the things you want to do. Depending on the frequency and nature of the commercialization, and your increasing skill set and resulting living efficiency, you may find you have cash left over which can be invested. That way, your passive income should increase in time with a resulting increase in lifestyle or decreased need for commercialization (depending on your fancy).

EXAMPLE
RIR RETIREES

Why should we be in such desperate haste to succeed, and in such desperate enterprises? If a man does not keep pace with his companions, perhaps it is because he hears a different drummer.

Henry Thoreau, 1854

It's helpful to look at actual case studies of people who have Radically Immediately Retired, without any planning.

Rachel (35) and Ben (38)

Rachel worked as an analyst and Ben a lawyer when they decided to Radically Immediately Retire. Rachel had no savings but an investment property with about $100,000 equity (and $300,000 debt). Ben owned 3 houses and an interest in his legal firm (with about $500,000 equity and $1,800,000 debt). Ben loathed his employment and it was affecting his health. Rachel could certainly imagine things she would rather be doing.

Both Ben and Rachel gave notice and put 3 houses up for sale. Ben also sold his interest in the legal business. This lead to both Ben and Rachel being debt free. Ben retained 1 house which was paid off completely (the house Ben lived in). He promptly rented this out for a return of $500 per week and both he and Rachel moved into Rachel's father's house. Rachel took the equity remaining from the sale of her house, and bought a small cottage outright in Europe.

So Ben and Rachel went from 2.1 million in dollars in debt between them (and an interest payment of over $10,000 a month) to no debt, an income producing asset and somewhere to live rent free in 3 months.

They lived in Ben's van for 8 months, travelling the country and having the time of the their lives, before moving to Rachel's new European cottage, where they now live rent free on the income from Ben's prior residence. They spend their time exploring the world and working on fun lifestyle businesses.

Thomas Backlund

Thomas had had enough. He quit his job, left his apartment, and went to live into the forest of Sweden, where he reduced his costs to almost zero and worked for 5 months on a new internet venture he was passionate about. After it got too cold for him he got a housesitting gig in the jungles of Costa Rica where he has continued to work on the project.[7]

Thomas is fit, happy and working on his passions with people around the globe.

Radical – for sure. But he's done it! And what a story. Would it be a better story if he sat depressed, gaining weight in his cubicle as he paid off a house in the suburbs?

Speaking of weight...

---

[7]   http://thomasbacklund.com/

Jason Mason

Jason was 27 years old worked as a second hand car dealer in the UK. He used to go out regularly and eat greasy UK food. He weighed almost 40 stone (250kg), and doctors had given him 5 years to live.

What was he to do? Continue with his crappy job and crappy lifestyle and put away 15% a year for his retirement at 65 (33 years after his expected death)?

No, Jason decided to retire from his nightmare existence. Radially and immediately. He sold everything and booked a one way ticket to Thailand and started training at a Thai kickboxing school. His expenses were very low and while it wasn't easy eventually he lost over 23 stone (150 kilograms) and now 'works' at the school as a trainer doing what he would be doing anyway – being fit![8]

You can't compare his life before and after RIR. His life was a misery and he was on the fast track to death. He could have kept working so he could pay for health insurance, or to pay for his mortgage, or to buy stuff at the mall.....

But what a waste of life that would have been.

You might have thought in each of these cases that the people involved took huge risks. That they 'got lucky'. But did they? Don't you think, given their brains and desires, that something else would have come up if the first choice didn't pan out? And, if in the unlikely worst case that they had a

---

[8]   See http://www.thephuketnews.com/british-man-loses-100kg-in-phuket-muay-thai-camp-35564.php.

total brain freeze and couldn't think of a way forward then what would they have done?

Gone back to their miserable lives.

See, no dramas. Just get another job – in the same area if that's all you're good for. They had nothing to lose. It may have been radical, but really, in the end it was pretty much risk free.

THOUGHTS
ON DEBT

Debt is the slavery of the free

Publilius Syrus circa 100 BC

Rather go to bed supperless, than rise in debt

Benjamin Franklin 1739

Some people feel paralyzed, trapped in their jobs – thinking it's beyond comprehension to leave - and they don't know why. Chances are they are in debt and they have normalized it.

Debt is a siren call. The way most of us have been raised leads to us wanting more more more. Credit cards and the like allow us to have it – now. Even if we have the smarts to not want to buy shit we can't afford (like a big TV), if you live beyond your means with respect to the small everyday stuff (like a night out on the drink) then you may well have none left over when the bills come in.

The temptation is to then pay the bills with debt and then continue your lifestyle (which now includes the minimum monthly payment). I must personally confess to buying a computer many years ago on a store card for $3,000. I dutifully paid off the $50 bill that came in every month for three years, before I called up to enquire as to my outstanding debt.

"$2900", was the answer.

I was gobsmacked. Three years of paying this little baby off had resulted in.... well, not paying any of it off. Minimum payments usually equals interest and nothing more.

What would I do now, with the benefit of hindsight? Well, don't buy the computer in the first place if you don't have the cash. Use someone else's (like the library's). Or I would buy a second hand one. Anything other than debt.

If I managed to convince myself that this investment was the ticket to freedom, then I would pay it back like it was my number one priority. As a greater priority than renting somewhere to live. A greater priority than going out for expensive big city drinks. A greater priority than anything other than staying alive at a campsite.

Debt starts with small purchases, which normalizes it. The behavior of others also normalizes it. There should be nothing normal about debt if you want to RIR. Debt is a chain around your neck. It makes the entirely possible appear entirely impossible. You should make clearing your debt your number one priority in getting out of the horror and retiring immediately.

How do you get out of debt? Imagine again you were advising a simpleton. What would you tell him or her to do to get out of debt. Then do it. The obvious stuff to sell is the stuff you don't want to sell. Forget the low hanging fruit. Sell the goddamn elephant in the room before you bother with the fruit.

Sell the house. Yes your precious house. Sell it - unless you can get someone else to pay the debt by renting it out. Sell it. Sell your car. Move somewhere you don't need a car, like a beach in Brazil, or close to the city, if you need to be in the city. If you really really really need a car, then use your big brain to work out what the cheapest old reliable enough car is. Then buy that one. If you have enough cash left over after you sell everything else.

Sometimes people can't sell their stuff to clear their debt. That happened to 'normal' people of Ireland before the 2009 financial crisis and property collapse. I personally know of a fellow who was earning 280,000 Euros when bought a million Euro house before the crash. It was only worth 300,000 Euros after.

Let's back up there. A person who was earning 280,000 Euro ($275,000) chose to risk it all on a one MILLION EURO house ($1,300,000)?

That's right. No, they didn't just invest the huge amount they could have saved each year (almost all of it). They didn't buy an affordable apartment or very small house, with cash. No, they leveraged up by borrowing over a million dollars, and ended up with an asset that was worth much less than half that. $600k plus down the gurgler in a couple of years. Working, for a lifetime, for.... nothing.

Did it matter though? Couldn't they just hang onto their asset as it was just their place of residence? Surely the market value is irrelevant? Well, it's irrelevant if you want to be locked into the once place *forever*, and are happy to be forced into working *forever*. This assumes, of course, a job that can make the repayments is available *forever*.

In the case of this fellow, it was not. Ireland was smashed in the face. Apart from the near collapse of the banking system, people were thrown out of work. This guy was. He was forced from his big fat $275,000 job into one paying just over $100,000. Sounds like a lot right?

Not when you have a million dollar mortgage.

What could this guy do? He went bankrupt, that's what. From the penthouse to the shithouse in a couple of years.

That's what debt can do to you.

For most of us it won't be this dramatic. Debt will simply chain you to your workplace, just as having expensive habits will chain you to your workplace. And if you prefer freedom to a cubicle, then you need to make some changes.

Speaking of which, what is freedom?

FREEDOM

Man is free at the moment he wishes to be

Voltaire, 1694-1778

*None are more hopelessly enslaved than
those who falsely believe they are free.*

Johann Wolfgang von Goethe, 1749-1852

Why do we even bother with this thinking? What is this 'Freedom' of which we speak, and why do we want it? Well, it isn't freedom to be fat and shoot guns. It isn't freedom to be ignorant. To me, it's freedom to do what I want with my time, which, really, is the only asset we have of any value, apart from our health and relationships with people.

Do you think you are free now because you have the cash to fly away with your partner once a month and blow a grand on a flash weekend? That isn't freedom. That's just State mandated rest so you return to work 'refreshed' after your two day break and earn more money to keep the economy and tax coffers ticking over.

True freedom is the ability to wake up and do as you choose for the day. You might have sex after you wake naturally (not when your precious sleep is smashed by an alarm) before getting up and taking the time prepare a healthy breakfast (not processed sugary garbage coming from a cereal box) before.....

Now what would take your fancy if you didn't have some overlord telling you how to perform like a seal almost *every waking moment of your adult life?*

If you are new to this freedom gig – and almost everyone is – then chances are you have almost destroyed your true self with your societal compliance so far. Who are you even? What *do* you enjoy? It may be that you don't know. You can think back to childhood dreams, but you aren't a child any more and they are likely to have changed. Your dreams at the moment may be consumption or income based, which is hardly the stuff of a life well lived.

It may take some time for you to work yourself out. Luckily, if you are truly free, then that's exactly what you have: time. Time initially, I suspect, to either relax and unwind or go wild, depending on your nature. Perhaps both. Don't deprive yourself of this. You deserve it. And, more importantly, you need it, after a lifetime of (self inflicted) abuse.

You might get sick in this initial period. People do, when they begin to unwind and de-stress. But it passes, and you will come back stronger. Over time, you will naturally get healthier as stress levels decrease and you have more time to spend outdoors, cook and generally look after yourself. It may take a couple of years for you to truly recover. You are likely to be unrecognizable by that time, both in appearance and how you view and interact with the world.

In terms of how to spend your days (a common concern, believe it or not), then the fact the question is asked shows how institutionalized so many have become. Chained by golden handcuffs and restrained by invisible bars, those that escape sometimes struggle with not being an inmate in today's forced labor camps.

What do you do with your time indeed.

If you truly need someone to hold your hand and tell you what to do all day, then track me down and I will get you to help me, for free, on my projects. God knows I have enough on the go (all mine, all free of negative stress).

Does that make you indignant? It should!

Do what you enjoy doing. As Tim Ferriss has said, it doesn't mean that you have to lie about all day having someone rub cocoa butter on your belly under a palm tree, although that is nice once in a while. Everyone is different, but for many pleasure comes through the mastery of skills, and creating things. You may learn how to ride a horse, or make a beautiful pot that doesn't crack when subject to temperature changes. Or perhaps you volunteer to look after puppies that have been abandoned by their mothers.

Whatever you do, you will naturally see opportunities for low stress commercialization of your interests. Take them if it suits. That's they key to RIR if you don't want to go caveman. Retire from the horror. Reduce your costs down to what you can afford given your assets and skills. And do what you please, taking advantage of opportunities that present themselves as you do.

Care must be taken not to resign from one nightmare only to create another. Only commercialize interests in a manner that is consistent with your ongoing enjoyment, and all the while retaining the ability to walk away without notice (preferably leaving a trailing revenue stream).

A persistent myth is that of 'doing what you love', as in building a career out of what you deemed interesting at age 17 and being financially dependent on you staying in it. Cooking up a scrumptious meal for 4 is completely and utterly different from being forced (in your own mind) to go into a hostile inferno every night for 40 years and cooking for 400.

Instead, you could be like Bill Buford, who wrote the excellent book *Heat: An Amateur's Adventures as Kitchen Slave, Line Cook, Pasta-Maker, and Apprentice to a Dante-Quoting Butcher in Tuscany*. The title pretty well gives it away, but essentially this guy was a journalist in his 50s who said screw it and quit his job and used his experience to get a year long gig cooking in a professional Italian kitchen, before travelling to Italy to seek more expert instruction in the arts of pasta making and butchery.

He then helped pay the bills from this awesome lifestyle by writing about it in the book. Next stop for him? France! To do the same with French cooking.

What a freaking awesome Radical Immediate Retirement!

Do you think he did it for the cash? No way! But he did it. He said "see ya!" to his masters and did something he enjoyed (which, Jacob Fisker might point out, involved a full time wage paying job) and then commercialized his hobby, in a way that he enjoyed. And the passive income will pay for the next phase.

Genius.

Does he have to slave away for the next 40 years with some 27 year old screaming at him? Nope. Nor does he have to be the screamer. But he can butcher a hog (he does in the book to the shock of his neighbours), make a mean pasta, and tell some brilliant stories, while all the while his book sales are ticking over – forever.

If you think you can't do something like this you're wrong. There has *never* been a better time to create passive income products and services over the internet. There are loads of books and articles out there telling you how to create your own podcasts, videos, books and location independent businesses. Forget the man. You're the man now, and you do with your time as you like, leveraging technology, exchange rates and global cost-of-living opportunities along with your ever increasing skillset to sidestep the miserable life of slavery the traditional (old person's) system has in store for you.

If you're shy you could get some traction before you cut the apron springs (and walk out into the bush to camp) – building up passive income or investments first. But really, if you use your big brain – really use it, like you're solving the biggest, most important problem of your life (which it is), then there is no reason why you can't retire right now. Immediately. Radically.

Once you do your only question will be why didn't you do it sooner.

MORE RADICAL MUSINGS

Join me at www.radicalimmediateretirement.com.

In terms of other sources, when the student is ready, the master will appear. What you are ready for, and which masters will appear, will depend entirely on you. That is what radical thinking is about!

Here are some sources that you might find helpful.

Early Retirement Extreme: A Philosophical and Practical Guide to Financial Independence
by Jacob Fisker

Jacob is the man. This book is worth buying even though it might do your head in in parts. Also check his blog out. Jacob advocates quickly accumulating sufficient capital to live forever on the returns by being frugal. Having said that he is a problem solver and no doubt would support someone working out how to Radically and Immediately Retire.

He also has a blog that you should read:
www.earlyretirementextreme.com.

Mr Money Moustache -
http://www.mrmoneymustache.com/

Mr MM also saved a bunch of cash quickly and lives off the returns after retiring at 30. He's better at PR than Jacob is, and perhaps less confronting, although their ideas are similar. He is also more accessible content wise.

The Four Hour Work Week by Tim Ferris

A complex, driven character who has a knack for marketing good ideas ahead of the curve. This book should help you if you want to be inspired to create a lifestyle business on the side and structure your life to avoid the grind.

Choosing Simplicity: Real People Finding Peace and Fulfillment in a Complex World by Linda Breen Pierce

Linda does a great job here examining real life examples of people who have made changes in their lives after a period of reflection.

Mind Over Medicine: Scientific Proof You Can Heal Yourself by Lisa Rankin

No, she isn't a nutter, she's a doctor taking a big picture approach. Your health and vitality problems may have more to do with your dysfunctional relationship or soul destroying job than anything else. The solution? Write your own prescription. Sign me up.

Made in United States
Troutdale, OR
12/05/2024

25936203R00029